YEAST of EDEN

YEAST of EDEN

POEMS THAT FERMENT THE SOUL

PROSENJIT NATH

AMARYLLIS

AMARYLLIS

An imprint of Manjul Publishing House Pvt. Ltd.
• C-16, Sector 3, Noida, Uttar Pradesh 201 301, India
Website: www.manjulindia.com
Registered Office:
• 2nd Floor, Usha Preet Complex, 42 Malviya Nagar,
Bhopal 462 003 – India
Distribution Centres
Ahmedabad, Bengaluru, Chennai, Hyderabad,
Kochi, Kolkata, Mumbai, Noida, Pune

Yeast of Eden: Poems That Ferment the Soul by Prosenjit Nath

This paperback edition first published in India in 2025

ISBN 978-93-5543-864-5

Printed and bound in India by Repro India Limited

In memory of Jayanta Mahapatra, whose quiet words echoed like monsoons in the soul of Indian poetry.

Contents

Inviting Words 1
Paradoxy 2
And so Today 3
First Day 4
Worth the Risk 6
Here, Now 8
Chronic 9
Nourishing Range 10
Words for an Old House 11
Sparrows 12
Birdless Cages 13
Crochet 14
Signs of Civilisation 16
Laundry 18
Tansy 19
Fireweed 20
Sage 21
Timing Is Everything 22
Benediction 23

Throw 24
Toad 25
Winged Thing 26
God of Peonies 27
Movement Is Also Meditation 28
Accommodations 29
Shoes 31
Small Living 32
Mosquitoes 33
Rain 34
Eleven Stones 35
Liminal People 36
Horticulturist 37
Breadcrumbs 38
Reconstruction 39
Feeding the Bears 40
Watershed 41
Oak Trees Die Quietly 42
Doors 43
Whole 44
Spent 45
Flying Lessons 47
Reason 49
Chin Up, Shoulders Back 50
Notes to Self 51

Leaning In 52
I Make My Own Bridges 54
Sand 55
Chronically Overwatering 56
Equinox 57
Despite Arguments from Rahi 59
It Begins 60
Biography 61
Good Light 62
A Ship Captain's Final Words 63
Swept 64
Highlight 65
Same Chapter, Same Verse 66
Consensus 67
Abridged Heroes 68
Initial Reaction 69
Nonsense 70
Be It Ever so Humble 71
Self Advocate 72
Wilderness 73
Some Days 74
Conductor 75
Momentum 76
Ontology 77
Open Your Eyes 78

Still Waiting 79
'I Need You' 80
The Sound of Words 81
Incongruous Heart 82
Significant Details 83
Window 85
Repairs 87
Murmuration 88
Unearned Beginnings 89
Subtitles 90
Cathedral 91
Ours 93
Variable 94
Yet 96
Waiting for Ice Out 97
Gaze Up 98
Unreasonable Expectations 99
Poetry Is Dead 100
Bloom 102
Two Words 103
Misplaced Affection 104
Milestones 105
Pearls 106
More or Less 107
Long Road 108

Empathy 109
Lightheart 110
Sauna 112
Playing with Fire 113
Broken 114
Plunge and Rise 116
Perfectionism 117
Those Three Words 118
Borrowed 119
Do I Love You? 120
Rose-Colored Glasses 121
Warming 122
Still Here 123
Swimming Laps on Saturday Mornings 124
Requirements 125
Spiral 126
Warm Spell 127
Retrospective 128
Joyfully 129
Drive 130
Distant 132
Light Fog 134
Downpour 136
Elevated 138
Gentle Rain 140

Life Bursts Forward 141
Fuel 142
Pulse 144
Always Close 146
Vital 147
Roadmap 148
Early Weekend 150
Relevance 151
Vision 153
Nothing 154
Immersion 156
Purification 158
Love Is a Stream 160

Inviting Words

When I am on an assignment and deadlines loom,
word counts rise like inescapable tides and I am tempted to
curse that blinking cursor. I
Dab perfume on my wrists.
At my throat. I coat my lips
in a shade of Parisian red, and I light candles.
I offer them haven—words that resist every other space
I've made for them on blank paper—and I simply listen.
I hear them tiptoe over the thresholds of my mind,
winding their way
into what needs to be said—what they've been waiting to say,
what I've been trying to convey, all this time, procrastinating
with too much force when in the end,
Everything longs for invitation.

Paradoxy

There's a tiny bit of poison
in every living thing—
Cyanide in apple seeds,
a sting in every bee.
But honey on the tongue,
can make it worth the risk.
Broken hearts from careless mouths
And still, a kiss on every lip.

And so Today

I will plant a tree,
anchoring hope in deepening roots
and new shoots rising skyward—home and
shade, shelter and air.
The world is on fire, and so, plant I must,
entrusting this fight against despair
to poems and to trees.

First Day

I should be used to this—we all should, really.
But 'should' is a wretched word.
Look at us, sending our hearts out
into the world, carefully shod in new shoes
and with bouquets of Ticonderoga pencils.
The sharpened edges of this past spring's education have
softened over the summer, and we send our apologies,
but the truth remains: we have loved so hard these short
months, cramming in every possible memory
and extended bedtime so we can stretch childhood that
much further.
Every minute matters, and now, as we flood feeds with
proof that we've tried—God we've tried—our best,
most of us are on our knees begging the world to be kind.
Please be so kind. These hearts of ours, sent out like this
are still fragile, despite their stiff upper lips and
shiny new backpacks.

We are all being so brave,
though we are both delighted by
and afraid of
everything
the world holds.

Worth the Risk

From where I sit this morning,
stuck in this dust-remembering body,
the morning is bright regardless. I have made coffee and
thrown open the windows as wide as they will go
even though I'm likely to allow entrance to wasps,
the same ones I found yesterday,
occupying the soul-gone body
of a small rabbit, its bare ribs revealed by cat's claws
and the hungry maws of insects.

I leave the windows open anyway.

Through them, I can more clearly see
the brilliant red heart of a Rose-breasted Grosbeak.
Now he opens his mouth and shouts melodies
at the sky. And I suppose, I
am working to remember:

The world is full of wasps
but also grosbeaks.
We are free to open windows.

Here, Now

Sometimes it's the smallest things:
A perfectly poached egg.
The smile of almost-recognition from a total stranger.
The bright scalloped edges of a late August zinnia.

'Aren't you glad you did not miss
this?' Croons the world.
'Aren't you glad you
are here,
Now?'

Chronic

Here is what I know about pain:
It insists on being felt and heard and known,
like a lonely child,
quiet and loud—simultaneously.
All-encompassing at times,
placated at others, aching to exist
where you did not issue invitation.
And you exist anyway. Choosing
to breathe and breathe through it,
smile and smile through it,
move on and onward with it until,
curiously, relief (however temporary) becomes
such an unfamiliar friend,
you frown at its occasional arrival—
like the ring of silence after
so much
Noise.

Nourishing Range

I stood today, in morning rain and
named every bird cry within a nine-mile radius,
which, is not only how far the human ear
can hear (and then some) but also how far a honeybee
forages, (though not in the rain) and,
I think it a curious coincidence that both
are true—as if the distance we creatures range
in awareness of our existence and the possibility of beauty
were not ironically synonymous
with the distance creatures range for food,
both after all, in the business of
nourishing.

Words for an Old House

Opening this door, I am greeted
with the warm breath of welcome. I have done
what I can to sustain and heal, sooth and
savour the time, the people, the bones made
and remade in these walls;
These walls respond in kind, time and time
again, holding and making space
for me. And as I leave and come, and leave again,
I bless and am blessed, kissing doorframes,
stepping lightly over thresholds.
This place, the face of a friend
I look forward to seeing again
upon return.

Sparrows

I finally located the nest
—empty now—
the song sparrow tucked into the garden, weaving
knife-sharp blades of grass into the safest place
she could, making home in wild places.
She was born to the practice.

Like a woman plunging hands into dishwater,
doing what needs being done, only to be bit
by the very blades she cleans.

We are made of more than feathers.
But watch us weave,
and bleed
and fly.

Birdless Cages

The spaces my smaller self once occupied have
since shrunk. I made doors as I grew
wings and practiced flying away from things
that no longer fit. And
it has recently dawned on me that this principle
always applies: time flies and ages, shrinking what once
felt right, until we are cyclically, seasonally forced
to lift brighter faces and gazes and feet and keep walking
through self-made doors, into
new rooms, shedding old selves and
old fetters.

Flight is a continuously-remembered practice,
useful only so long as it is used in a life
filled with skies peeled open
and the hope of birdless cages.

Crochet

I am teaching my daughter to crochet,
though, I barely know the way of it myself.
This is to say, I am also teaching my daughter to weave and
untangle the knots of herself, making something
Lovely, hopefully. Useful, hopefully. Good, already.
Even as I also, am learning.

Make a looped knot, and then
let the needle find the thread,
but turned away from you—secretive,
snagging while you hold the tail tight. Turn the needle and
reveal the prize, caught, as you pull it through
so gently, and there: A single loop.

This repeated, will gather a collection
over time, through infinite practice until
Something is made. It's hard to tell what, now.
But in time, something
Lovely, hopefully.
Useful, hopefully.
Good, already.

Signs of Civilisation

According to Margaret Mead,
it is the intentional mending of a femur,
which identifies humane civilisation, and not
fire, or tools.

I emptied my pockets at the close of the day:
A rumpled Downy woodpecker feather.
An agate, collected by my daughter.
A tiny, gold, star-tipped drill bit.
I am repairing the leg of a small desk—
found second hand, skeleton key
intact.
Incidentally, it matches a different found skeleton key,
for which I had an entire desk made.

This smaller sister, once mended, will
offer creative purchase for new words in
new spaces, and
I can think of nothing more whole nor humane than this:
To mend and make whole every found thing
fit with found keys, for which locks
were dreamed and opened wide,
for the sake of good words.

Laundry

I found a blue jay feather caught
in the lint trap as
I changed out the laundry;
remnants of remembered wings,
shed by my children,
perhaps.
I smoothed it out, zipping it
between thumb and forefinger,
the way you crease a seam.
One never knows
when one might need
a tidy feather.
The sky
is calling.

Tansy

Have you noticed, lately
the brightness of yellow tansy?
How it grows where it will,
unhindered by fence lines and
boundaries?
I have taken to carrying it with me,
pinning it to my lapel. So fierce, and
self-contained, and
free.

Fireweed

The place where I burned debris
last fall has burst into colour, here
in the heat of July.
Fireweed, phoenix-like, flames purple where
the ground was charred
past recognition.
Perhaps birth is always a kind of death
at first. Time works wonders
in all burned
ground.

Sage

I have left
the small patch of wild sage
growing between the cracks
on my front walk.

Joy is the one emotion
I do not navigate with
dexterity, I am distrusting
of its constancy—far more familiar
with grief.

And yet, joy, like sage
springs up in unruly places
demanding to live.
And how it seasons
the very air
I breathe.

Timing Is Everything

It's always growing, this green
fruit. Part of a process I can only
experience upon summer's end. But
all the while, the tree is at work—
sunlight and rain, winter snows and
soul-draining dry spells—
each contributing to the
eventual ripening sweetness,
ready in its own
perfect
time.

Benediction

I am saging Summer, taking my turn and
lighting this match at the dawn of the day—
saying Words over the water. I'll be a token,
spokesperson (if you wish) for
every daughter who is fighting her way towards
a quiet summer, only to discover
she has to carry This now, too.
Let me eschew, if I may, that mindset,
that stuck-ness. Let me set
aside, with you, this moment.
Let smoke rise, let morning have her say
on new dreams, new themes and ways
of being whole—wholeheartedly here,
in the now. Let peace rain, and reign,
and we will make our way
forward, not alone.

Throw

I have a daughter who loves to throw
things with such abandon and joy—
Balls and stuffed toys and
the occasional glass bottle on trips to
the landfill. And I refuse to curb her
elation. For, how much better that she lean
into the thrill of her body's strength, her
ability to scatter shards
(in designated places) and to gather
distance with each endeavour,
than to throw herself
away in effort to meet other's
expectations.

Toad

She crouched, long-shadowed
in the porchlight, unencumbered by
herself; suited to slow movement, and
shady spaces, the quiet dark, and dinner.
I stroked her back, gently, praising her ways,
promising to make them
my own.

Winged Thing

It's okay to grieve the things
you hoped for.
Hope is no small thing, Love,
nor you, and grief is proof
it mattered. It matters still
always will and
here you are, tears watering
this good ground
Rise. Up you get.
There is much to be now
that you are done with
what once was. Hold it all
in open hands, Love.
Hope is a winged thing,
remember?

God of Peonies

Now, whenever I find myself forced up against
the insistence that god exists in
masculine framework only, I laugh and
think of peonies.
The wild extravagance. The superfluous generosity.
The foolish gorge of beauty thrown into singular stems.
As if an Entity with this kind of imaginative scope
could only ever be a single thing. Such thinking
prefers god small, fixed and fundamentally
convenient. Pocket-sized.
I am certain
of more lavish, more nurturing, more wasteful Muchness,
(even for beauty's sake alone)
than small, safe, singular
definitions
would allow.

Movement Is Also Meditation

I read this somewhere
last night, between one and four am,
I don't remember where but
it was deeply comforting. I
can't seem to stop moving
these days. Even when my body decides
she's had enough, my mind refuses to give up.
I've been practising focusing my motion,
measuring my steps,
anchoring my hips a shoulder's width
apart as I step-step-step several miles at a time.
There is rhythm to it; rhyme,
my breath aligning as I move over the ground,
my shadow close as I anchor my pace,
listen to my breath,
and meditate.

Accommodations

I used to imagine there was,
somewhere out there, someone
looking for me—
someone who fit against the exact edges
of the space I occupied
in the world. And when
we found one another, there would be a kind of gasping
relief—
'At last! There you are!'

These days, I am finally aware that space expands,
around us each. Not to accommodate,
but because Need alters.

And, it's a breathless thing to discover
after all this time that
I need not wait for the space of another's Need
when I am already enough
for my own.

Shoes

I walked a mile
in my own shoes
today.

I still have scars from the
blisters yours gave me.
They still ache, and
I would not trade them
because now I know how that
feels. But—

I guess what I'm saying is,
maybe we could go for a walk sometime,
together. Each of us in our own shoes.
Neither of us alone.

Small Living

Tonight we are living small,
curled in on one another shoreside
with the wind at our backs,
all the light ambient.
Bright Eyes croons from
the old radio atop the refrigerator,
'This is the first day of my life—'
and it might as well be,
because it all feels right tonight
small, and good, and briefly
whole.

Mosquitoes

I killed three
vampires tonight.

Let not their small size
fool you. They will suck
the last drop
of sanity from your
much-craved rest.

It's for the best.
Their deaths will not
be mourned.

Rain

I didn't realise I
was waiting for the rain
until it began to fall
tip-tip-tip on
the pavement, and I
tripped over myself in my
rush to stand in the deluge.

Let it assuage every parched part
I let dry out accidentally.
Let it set things back in motion
which drought and doubt dried,
until the knots I laced in the
shoestrings of my heart
loosen.

Let it rain on
my barefoot soul.

Eleven Stones

Don't break bones,
or kill birds.
Let them be for skipping only.
I am trying to avoid being trapped
between one, and hard places, and
if I succeed I'll let you know.
Keep them in pockets, and
refuse to live beneath them.
Let your word be carved,
your song be heard,
your heart lighter always. And
may you find what you're looking for—
each one turned over.

Liminal People

She sits across from me sipping
an Old Fashioned, neat, and leaning
into our conversation, her very self—a
doorstop holding
space and keeping open
a way between—
'Let me be a space where
you can stand, and I'll hold your heart
on the way,' she says with
her eyes
her voice
her leaning in.
How marvellous, that liminal
people exist. Fluid, sometimes
lonely, waiting rooms for every
part
of every heart
they hold.

Horticulturist

I repot the plants
that withered through winter—
hands in soil, mind
drifting between yesterday
and the pulse of now.
How much care is too much?
How deep should the roots go?
Did I drown them again
in my trying?
What I need
is a rain gauge for the heart—
maybe for my whole life.
I walk these bones
still unsure
of where to stand,
how much to hold.
It's both mercy and misfortune
that these plants live in pots
at all.

Breadcrumbs

I dream recklessly about personal
sustainability and gaps in my soul
that are no longer empty. I search painstakingly
for parking lot pennies, which
the world mostly misses, too preoccupied
with urgency to remember the buoyancy
of tiny accumulating pocket change.
I have changed too much to go back.
I would rather lack bread loaves in my pantry
than keep scrabbling after breadcrumbs
of joy. Life is too short for the sort of nonsense
that leaves us content to lick knife blades
instead of taking seats at the tables
we build ourselves.

Reconstruction

May is uncurling
herself the tender edge
of a silver birch leaf
sticky and fragile but
plumb with potential.
And here I am, a scavenger,
winter-starved and wild for
the colour green,
nipping at buds with broken teeth,
my heart aching and open,
rebuilding my very bones
from the almost forgotten framework
of a budding season.

Feeding the Bears

A bear tore into the bird feeder last night,
bending the metal frame, curling it inward,
releasing sunflower seeds like rain
into the newly greening grass.
She fed herself freely first, and then her cubs,
taking without apology,
leaving claw marks as her signature.

I traced those marks with my fingertips this morning,
glad she enjoyed, glad she savoured,
glad she left her name as proof.

I wish more women feasted so—
unapologetically and with joy.

Watershed

When it rains like this
I let my mind trace old landscapes.
I too am glacier-hollowed and
mounded by moraine.
There is room for what water lingers
before seeping into newly-soft soil.

An early morning song-sparrow emphasises
hope ensconced in feathers as the sun rises
beneath cloud banks, and
the quenching sky soothes,
mapping watersheds of my
topographical heart.

Oak Trees Die Quietly

From the inside—
secret and understating what is later
obvious, leaving casual observers oblivious
until they begin to self-consciously shed limbs.
Though, by then, it's really too late.
Meanwhile, they still leaf out in the spring,
still offer acorns, still stretch skyward
all, while on the inside, they quietly
hollow and hollow out.
Heaven forbid they inconvenience anyone
with their eventual absence—
with their eventual absent spread
of so much crowning
shade.

Doors

I am in the business
of making doors
and repairing them.
Holding doors ajar.
Occasionally, closing them
and holding them
shut.
I am, in fact,
myself a door even
as I also walk through.
Though, I am only just
realising this.
This is, perhaps,
the most definitive word for
woman,
that I know.

Whole

exists only
because of each
and every broken
part.

We spring from our parts—
made

and those we make,
spring from theirs.
And from ours.

The best we can hope for,
truly, is to be and become,
wholehearted.

Spent

The cupped sand curls
a wash of water
around his fragmented self.
And I crouch,
running one fingertip
along the ridge of his leathered back.

What must it be like
to be the last of something?
Counting your kind back
eons? Washing
up on southeastern shores
for longer histories
than my kind
can count?

Look at the gentle palm of the shore,
so tender with spent stories.

Flying Lessons

I am trying to say things I don't have words for—
What I mean is,
have you ever dreamed of flying?
Discovered you had wings, (or arms that worked as wings),
and they saved you, at the very last moment?

Sometimes I save myself, but
most often I save others—I don't know
what this means, save, perhaps,
I am aware . . . no. Awake to heartache.
It's loud, you see? What am I trying to say?

I can fly. Or maybe I knew how, once.
Once upon a time there was girl who remembered—

Words have power. I tell my children this,
and I have taught them how to swear. Proper usage. Context.
The world is too much not to have the words we need.

What is it I need? I don't have the words.
Flying lessons, perhaps.
I've given all my parachutes away.

Reason

I am standing here shaking,
over the way every report is
emphasizing
how smart
and achieving
and kind
and respectful
and decent
each non-white victim is.
Every time.

As if being human
with skin
is not enough reason
not to
shoot.

Chin Up, Shoulders Back

I find it amusing,
the way my body straightens unconsciously
frame aligning, spine finding
centre
the moment someone mentions
posture.
I forget to let myself be seen,
curling in automatically
unless prompted
otherwise.

I see you too,
are taller now. Remembering.
Centre found.
Welcome back.

By the way,
I love your crown.

Notes to Self

When I was a girl
I would write notes for
the future owner of my house,
hiding them between the floorboards and
in cracks in the walls, never imagining
it would be me, finding them.
And now, as I patch broken bits of trim, or
replace a window sash, and
find notes to my unsuspecting self
written on old letterhead,
in my own childish way,
I wonder if she—that girl I was—knew
the girl I am now would need those words:
'Life is good and you are brave'
all these years later.

Leaning In

I have moved my bed closer
to the window, hauling open the sash, despite the cold.

These past few nights I have lain in the dark
watching the slash of the moon wax wider.

Though the snow lingers, songbirds have returned
and the whisper-cry of the nighthawk encourages me

to take stock of my soul, in the pre-dawn hours.
Legends say she looks after such things.

And now, the light seeps over the eastern edge
of everything, detailing the orange breast of

a robin, assisting the rise of the sun
with his song.

And I lean in, soul open. I've been waiting so long
for spring.

I Make My Own Bridges

Here, in the middle of the story it's hard to remember
that change is a bridge I build myself, when
it feels like a canyon, yawning, devouring, slaughtering
hope, or at least, my too-small version of it.
More often than not I must knot my own ropes.
At least then I am assured they will hold. And if they do fold
beneath my weight, I've only myself to own,
and I can remake them as I grow incrementally stronger.
I'll build it back better—wider, longer—enough for others.
Change both burns and builds these bridges,
strung from ridge to ridge, from life to life.
and the princess is strong, and stronger-willed than
Once Upon a Time.

Sand

I am gathering up
these days,
grains of sand from my own
personal hourglass,
and pocketing them.
I'll carry them with me.
Some will get lost—
in the laundry, perhaps.
Some I'll give away—
remembered treasure for others to pocket.
And some I'll take out and
hold in my palm.
Look how they glitter now
in all this light.

Chronically Overwatering

They tell me succulents are easy to keep
alive, but

when you strive constantly
not to overwater and are prone to drowning
plants (and people) in all this excess assistance with
living, giving

more than you should,
and forgetting to save some for yourself—
well,

it's easier to keep potted ferns,
alive, always eager for a drink,

and wear, rather than water,
a string of pearls.

Equinox

Sometimes, when I can't sleep,
I play this game wherein I contrive solutions to
every possible crisis that could arise,
racing through my life like
a dark horse, which of course is mania and
excellent fodder for therapy,
and also, perpetual insomnia.

Trauma preparedness aside, this mental review also points
me in directions of small joy, for one cannot envision crisis
without first noting its absence.

The quiet night, for example.
The elegant turn of the earth on its balanced axis.
The steady heartbeats beneath my shared roof.

All these, proof of how little is actually dependent upon
me, and the relief—
like the long-awaited dawn.

Despite Arguments from Rahi

Last year, this time
the Thyme was reaching brown twigs
towards the sky,
making grand promises in shades of green.
And from between the remaining
banks of snow cover,
the rhubarb was pressing forward
through the cold.
But today, this old winter still firmly grips
my garden,
despite arguments from Rahi
and from me.

It Begins

This morning I stood barefoot
beneath the brightening tent of the sky
and arched my body into the sound
of a robin singing
the dawn into being,
sending his longing
into the world,
and giving voice
to mine.

Biography

I protest sometimes the part
I've been assigned—this physicality,
all these bones and the curtain
of the scene draped just
so, over the known and
unknown parts—
this heart made of stories,
made of darkness and light, and then
after all that,
certain finality.

And yet, how else would I rise,
wrapping hands around my warm cup,
than in this body,
the buttery light of March's morning sun
casting the certain shape of my kind shadow
against the wall.

Good Light

I've been standing in this skin—
the thick and the thin of it
for my whole life, and it's beginning
to tell lovely stories, truths
about who and where and how I've been. And
the collection of lines, like
script on a page, no longer concerns me
as once it did. These lines are my proof,
my framework for a wholehearted way
of staying, and staying true—
of choosing me, after not quite doing so
for far too long.
Shadows aren't conducive to life, And so,
I'm shifting my stance, sliding out of corners—
no walls against my back, standing
taller, brighter, kinder, wiser,
in this good light.

A Ship Captain's Final Words

I see you found my heart, my Love
it finally washed ashore—
the edges smoothed, softened
more than I could have managed
without the pull of the tide,
and the steady brush of sand to soothe.
The sharp-eyed gulls have picked it clean,
leaving here, my heart bone.
It's yours to carry. To pocket, if you will.
My frantic, fervent, restless heart
is finally, blissfully
still.

Swept

The crest and crash of foam and tide
rides the cry of whatever nameless thing
lives in me, responding mindless
to the sea.
And I cannot decide
if it is harder here
to stay,
than to let myself be swept
by waves.

Highlight

I saw the sun this morning, briefly.
It touched everything, gilding,
wielding significance like a benevolent god
elegant in the way she highlights,
makes prominent, the most ordinary
things.

Same Chapter, Same Verse

I'm taking my favourite piece of this
day (of everyday, really)
and replaying it
until my bones ring—
until everything sings—
with that resonance
you spoke into the light when you woke.
Those sweetest words.
Only three.
I spoke them back to you
in reverse, as I always do, like a question
and you nodded.
Same chapter
Same verse
on a constant loop,
mixed, remixed, fixed in my mind.
A song I'll insist on replaying
every day from now until
always.

Consensus

I saw a greeting card yesterday that read,
'There's no good card for This,' and
the irony of that spoke to more
than well-meant empathetic wishes
probably bore testament to.
There were only four cards stocked and
I bought them all, disappointed, as
I need approximately seven billion nine hundred
ninety-nine million nine hundred
ninety-nine thousand nine hundred
ninety-six
more
in this universal agreement
that the world could use a
bit more encouragement.

Abridged Heroes

If we truncate our stories
choosing to skip from one
heroic act to the next,
arriving at the page with
only partial truths,
we aren't made heroes, rather
false historians
content to bridge our brokenness
rather than honour our hearts
while blithely abridging the tale.

Initial Reaction

Even a casual observer will note
the world is on fire, and
everyone I know
is desperate for water.
But the well is dry. Still,
I keep dredging the bottom,
dragging up sand and silt,
smothering what flames
I can.

This morning, a cardinal stands on tiptoe
from the tallest tip of the sky-scraping maple
just beyond my front door,
singing, singing, singing
the flaming sun over the rim of the day.

His red body is stark against the sky
and weary as I am,
thirsty as I am,
my initial reaction is relief.
Even now
the world
sings.

Nonsense

Sitting here in the paved stillness,
somewhere between school pickup and
evening routine.
My overcoat is overly warm but
March is overly cool and overhead
a troupe of Jays protests the nonsense
of it all.
These are the moments
where my life happens—
in the between, while waiting
for The Next Thing.
But if you ask the Jays, they will be
happy to tell truths about the sky,
so blue, and so full of
only now and
now and
now.

Be It Ever so Humble

In the quiet night when sleep evades,
I can feel the house curl into herself,
purring and wrapping around me, cat-like.
I run my fingers along the curved stair-rail of her spine,
barefoot on my way to the kitchen.

There, we listen to the wind
throwing himself against the windows,
trying to get in, gnashing teeth at me while I make tea.
The house ignores him—a barking dog
she is too self-assured to acknowledge.

At night, with my tea, and the company of memories
in this place that has held me steady for so long
I wrap hands around my cup
and curl my body close as
the good bones of this place
stand sturdy and sound,
sweet.

Self Advocate

On my good days
I fight for her, choose her,
refuse to lose her to
pity or weary apathy.
On my good days
I refuse to sit down and play small
I rise up, climb up, and show up for all
the past versions of her and
the ones yet to come.
But sometimes,
I wish I could just
rest while
someone else
advocated
for me.

Wilderness

When I was small, my father taught me to
find my way in places ways were scarce.
I learned the constancy of stars and the
certainty of sunrise in the dark. Moss is an unreliable guide,
but deer paths always lead through the thick of things, and
birds sing both at dawn and dusk.
And if you know how to trust your own senses
in the dark, being lost is little more than a temporary
inconvenience, for nothing is lost forever.
I think he meant to give me security in the world,
but when I was a child, my father gave me the wild,
and tools to navigate it unafraid.
These days, when the wilderness is more a matter
of navigating callous hearts, it's nice to know
I can still find my way in the dark.

Some Days

Some days drag
at all the hollow places—
the spaces you left open,
hoping light would filter in but instead
all these shadows—
echoes of longing
you don't have a name for.
It leaves an ache unsatiated by
anything you offer it.

Some days you must simply sit
with the hollowness and
make it hallowed—
let it prove to your
moved and unmoved soul
that you aren't Home yet.

Conductor

What is music if not note after note
plucked from pre-existence, and
thrown against the page,
sent back to the universe, newly ordered?

They say everything sings,
each moiety of matter, from the grandest planets
to the smallest atom
vibrates at its own frequency.

And so, what is everything
if not part of a grand orchestra?
And what is music if not
the orchestration of careful order?

An ode to the joy of sound
delightfully, intentionally
conducted.

Momentum

If you lean into the wind
you will invariably meet
the places it has been
before you—
the way it has carried
flurry, flotsam, and the fragrance
of the world
to your doorstep—
simply by opening it up
and stepping out.

Ontology

Sometimes, I step out into the cold,
barefoot in the snow to feel
the burn and to watch my own mind,
fall on the knife-blade knowledge of herself.
To witness the clear line of my own *is-ness*.

There: the edge of the world and
the snow, iced water, so soft and so sharp.

There: the edge of me and
my own softness, my obsession
with comfort and warmth.

And then I step back inside, the lines of myself,
my own mortality, blurring again
as certainty is stroked by wool socks and
the gentle heat of the fire.

Open Your Eyes

If you ever struggle, hands out before you
looking for your way in the dark
it's okay. You're not alone.
Some of the most beautiful things
in eternity are still here.
Don't be afraid.
Open your eyes, Love.
See?
There are so
many
stars.

Still Waiting

I woke up to sun today, and the reminder that March is historically, the most extravagant giver—
More snow in the forecast.

I am trying not to be downcast by this news because the truth is, here, Spring is hard won. And I'll likely never be done throwing words against the page about that. It resonates with me too deeply. This reality: Months of waiting, frozen in the dark while the planet slowly tilts, and we try to hold onto whole hearts while our whole beings lean into the shift like sun-starved things.

When we wait with expectation, there is a certain kind of action tied up in everything—A heightened knowing, a sowing, almost as if in waiting we will also make the change.

'I Need You'

A life of being needed
implies endless purpose
but the paradox is this:

Those who become too invaluable
allow others to be incapable
of everything but need.

Let me be wanted
but not needed
from now on. Chosen
for my company
rather than
my service
only.

The Sound of Words

I am in love with the resonant tones
of the human voice and
the way we wrap sounds
around meaning and lean into one another
to better convey the weight of our words—
their power ever at odds with the frailty of
the world and us in it—always on the threshold
of life and death.

I remembered the moment I discovered
that a mere twenty-six letters combined
lent themselves to worlds upon worlds.
And so, I learned to read and read aloud,
the sound of my own voice tripping over language,
fascinating and full of a found-ness I had never known prior.
And now I cannot dam them up,
these words, as if the need to hold
memory and experience and emotion
is as desperate as held breath beneath the surface
and I am always gasping—grasping
for just the right ones.
And the sound of those rightly found:
Like air.

Incongruous Heart

I want you out there
in the middle of the wild
rush and rise of living—
Discovering, enjoying, remaking
this whole wide world, and
I want you here
safe and found, every part.
Such is the war of my
incongruous heart.

Significant Details

I am too easily caught up
in the grandiosity of things—
The pine-peaked ridge of the landscape,
like teeth of a shadowed beast.

The migration patterns of songbirds,
ever unfailing but ever in flux.

The cosmic dance of stars,
never stagnant but sure enough
to steer ships by

And the way elephants remember.
Remember.
Remember,
when I cannot.

Why must it matter so—
what we had for dinner last night
when the world tilts
and we are still here,
despite all that speed and gravity?

A single moment's pause
would cause us all to fly into

oblivion

All that
beef stroganoff untasted.

Window

I found a window in this old house
that I never knew existed—
covered over by ivy so dense
everything was obscured.
Especially the light.

It took some doing—
pulling it all back,
cutting the vines,
repairing the facade.

The window is free now
and I throw it open so
fresh air and light
may galivant down the hall.

But ivy is nothing if not persistent.
I must cut it back often, and
if I am not careful,
if I'm not paying attention,
one-leaf-after-another
s l o w l y
the light is
gone.

'Wasn't there a window here?' you ask
after some time.
The halls have begun to forget

the memory of fresh air
of light . . .

'There was!' I say, remembering.
You offer your pruning shears,
and help.

Repairs

I have lived my whole life, here,
rebuilding and remaking,
uncovering every lovely thing,
awakening what was lost and under-loved
for far too long.

I have stripped back floorboards and
straightened stairwells,
reframed doorways and added windows
where they were always meant to be,
letting her breathe
again.

Houses, like people, are at their best
when known and loved—
the broken places honoured with attention
and all the lovely time-earned imperfections,
bathed in light.

Murmuration

Roadside starlings rose up as
we drove by, in
a flurry of wings and words
I haven't learned yet.

They've carried them and
each other across landscapes
I've never seen,
murmuring flighted stories
in cacophonous singing.

And I can only lean in
and wish for wings.

Unearned Beginnings

This space, made of
silent symphonies and pastel hues speaks
to my soul like a cloud of witnesses.
I am caught up and overcome by
the sun that rests just there,
rising over the edge of the world unhurried,
unencumbered by the comings and goings,
all these unknowings of us.
It is enough to simply shine, and in so doing
alter the course of things for this galaxy.
Perhaps, others as well, unbeknownst to me,
seeing only smally from my place in it.
Regardless, I am certain
dawn will always draw awe out of me
knowing I am here, watching, bathed in light
my own body casting long shadows freely.
It could have been anything really, at every turn,
but it is warmth and light,
and unearned beginnings.

Subtitles

It would be so useful,
If we all arrived with subtitles.
shrugs

Imagine meeting someone for the first time
and never having to wade through rhyme or
guess if the words they spoke
beautiful, articulate
matched their hearts without having to evoke
hopeful wit
on your part.

Cathedral

I am awfully tired
of cathedrals constructed
to call out my smallness,
my meagre substance,
my minor station,
as if God
was ever overly concerned
with an inability to remedy these.

That work is done and finished.

The One who fixed stars and
set northern lights as spires
in the heavens,
Who erected pines and offered me
a carpeted aisle of moss
for a bare-footed traipse towards worship
is far more concerned with
the condition of
my heart than with the size
of the fellowship hall.

And the fall of man, I think,
will be ushered in
on silver offering plates
while God waits
out here in the wild
with kids
like me.

Ours

I find it fitting
that ships are named after women.
Feminine too, the oceans they traverse and
the land they leave behind.
Estates and abodes, empires and even
the earth herself.
And rightly so.
For what woman hasn't carried and held,
(willingly and otherwise)
multitudes?
We usher life and uphold it
though it has cuffed and anchored,
ravaged and disregarded the gift
more often than not.

But these days, I see us studying
our birthrights with great care,
christening our bows with marvellous intent,
and embarking—remembering:
The seas were always ours.

Variable

Things could go either way.
That's the implication.

So, you try—
you try so hard
to make them sway
and lean favourably in your
direction.
You do all the right things.
All the right words in all the right voices,
all the right choices.

Even so
they go sideways.

Over and under byways—
That's where your heart lives now,

taking backroads, and
living off the broken loaves
of someone else's miracles.

There's always enough until there isn't,
right? But that's the plight
of belief. And I'll never trade it.

There's still so much relief housed in Hope—
the reach itself a form of arrival.
Salvation in the variables.

Yet

Yet is such a small word.
Both adverb and conjunction,
connection and comparison:

The landscape was ensconced in shadow,
Yet I've never seen
the moon so bright.

Also—

Sometimes I'm astonished
that I haven't Yet fallen
more in love with the darkness
and the way she pulls my heart
towards rest.

Waiting for Ice Out

Though we are tipping towards a new solstice
it's easy to imagine this
will last forever—every soft
and moving ripple, numb and sealed
beneath silent chill.

If I think too long about oxygen-hungry fish,
biding their time while
light-starved aquatic plants wither,
I begin to gasp slightly
on their behalf.

But time has taught me that even a slow sun
warms, and
every ice-bound
thing finds thaw
eventually.

Gaze Up

When clouds close overhead and
my collarbones tilt toward the ground
without my permission,
I am determined still, to keep all of this grey
in remission—
uncurling my hunched
soul, slowly unfolding my fists, and
lifting my face to the bowl of the sky.

I remember the first time I realised
stars shine day-side,
regardless of my ability to see them,
and something within me woke and spoke aloud
to that view of so many bright unseen stars—
as blazing an invitation
to still gaze, and gaze up,
as any.

Unreasonable Expectations

If we could just not forget—
this need that lies alongside our bones,
curled around the coil of our DNA,
winding through sinew and thought—
without second thought, so that
we can exist without wondering if we
know-see-believe-love-remember
one another.

Poetry Is Dead

they say,
and I pray it isn't true.
I've been writing words along my bones and
they help me stand a little taller
forcing these shadows to shrink
on this long walk home.

I'm gathering up handfuls— syllables
that sound like songs to me
and breaking down the complexities
of this whole wide world so, I can hold on
and hold it in the palms of my heart
a little better.

Besides, the mortality rate of words
feels like a thing hinging on attempts
to be only clever, when what I need better,
is to invite others in—
offering up the places where the scars
on my heart look like yours.

And if that makes me an unwieldy worker of all these words,
at least they no longer live alone in either of our heads,
and we can both be prophets and storytellers
before poetry is confirmed dead.

Bloom

Today I need flowers—
the languishing drama of aging tulips and
the reckless flash of yellow daffodils.
I need bright heavy-headed ranunculus, and
the extravagant fragrance of peonies. Give me
lilacs and the lunacy of blue delphinium. I want
to lay myself down beside the faces of violets, and
place the pale blooms of clover on my tongue,
savouring every drop of sweetness.
The world has been colourless for far too long.

Two Words

When the otherness of everything and
the weight of Being, seeps
like water over a floodplain, abandoning its banks
I write words in the palms of my hands:
Hope and Grief.

I clap them together, dusting flour while baking bread, and
I hold the faces of my loved ones between them,
kissing away the pain of knowing, seeing, tasting too much.
I clench them around the frailty of my own body
prone to flying apart in storms, and
I raise them to my eyes,
cupping a keyhole through which
I view this lovely broken-hearted world.

It is enough for me
to focus my gaze,
loving widely, holding the world
gently, gently, gently
between hope and grief.

Misplaced Affection

If my younger self had avenue
for choosing an easier route,
a smaller mountain,
a calmer sea,
she would have taken it.
Without question.
But the struggle through,
that upward climb,
those waves,
made me.
Perhaps preferring easy roads
is misplaced affection.

Milestones

One, two, you've skipped a few
across the water, even—
Three, four, throw some more
at what you believe in.
Five, six, set your hope
and get up every morning—
Seven, eight, scale the gate
and show them what you're learning.
Nine, ten, keep digging in
It's life you're undertaking—
Eleven, twelve, there you are
One more year in the making.

Pearls

I relieved them of their pearls
as they would not quit
clutching them. And
I put them in my mouth,
grinding them between my teeth
over time.
And now as I speak
they fall to the floor.
Pearl dust
before swine.

More or Less

Look at the way you shine, there,
in the light
in my mind
sometimes more
sometimes less

And yet.

It's time
I stop embracing you
for what I know you are capable of being,
and believe you when
you show me who you are.

Long Road

Give me words that make me weep
and forget to draw breath or

Draw it so sharply that people
sneak a glance across the aisle.

I refuse to settle for a gasp-free life, empty of
awe and shock and wonder and rage.

I will throw myself into this restless urge for wider
spaces, and greater graces than we have been yet afforded.

In what ways I have had to earn for myself,
I will grant others freely, crafting

Keys for every locked door and gate
because this is the truest truth I know:

The road is long, and we cannot walk home limping,
wordless, voiceless, or alone.

Empathy

For so long the volume on this
song has been turned up past
bearing, no turning it down could drown out
the ring in my mind or the kind of pain it
amplified as I pushed through days needing
a single moment's reprieve for my bleeding
heart.

And, living in the Valley amplifies echoes.
There is no escape, no mountaineering climb
nor sudden break for it, when peaks offer only
higher pitch.
I was left with the choice:
To lance my own ears and shut out the sound, or learn to
dance.

Here now in the centre of
the Already and the Not Yet I am
learning the steps. Living with the noise
of the world and the noise of my heart—
moving, swaying, making room
still whole and still torn apart.

Lightheart

For every time you crawl up the face of this
nameless broken landscape
following a course someone else set
I hope you know,
you're the bravest, kindest, strongest person
I've ever watched wrestle through.

And when they close the doors on you
despite acknowledging all those hoops
I want you to know I'm eager to engage and
happy to burn the whole thing down.
Even when you tell me it isn't worth it,
that they haven't earned my rage.

Well, they haven't earned you either.
And I'll shout that through every keyhole,
through every shut door, on every front porch.
Your brightness isn't dimmed though they've
been happy to hide it and tear it apart.

No amount of their darkness can dim
your own glorious and chosen lightheart.

Sauna

I am curled into the dark tonight
Northern winter wrapping herself
around the ridge pole of this small warm room.
The fire blazes and I've lit candles
as my grandmother's people
would have done.
Steam fills the air and my skin prickles
under its touch, sweat pooling in
the hollow beneath my throat.
Birch and lavender fill my lungs and a
thousand tales wrap themselves
around my bones in this heat—
part comfort, part medicine, party story.
And I am glad for the ways my people, and
my people's people carved their lives
from ice and stone and memory
offering me a legacy of
steam-wrapped dreams
to build this life upon.

Playing with Fire

There are sparks buried in my bones.
Warm ash lines the back
of my throat and I have banked coals
in that space between sinew
and strength where heat roils and roars.
I may not look it,
but I am accustomed to flames.
And I suggest you do not play
with me,
lest I burn
and burn
and burn.

Broken

'Broken things grow back stronger.'
I've heard that said. And true or false
the marvel lies largely in the first part:
Broken things grow.

In this tour de force through life,
the audacity of my existence
and the audacity of yours are, of course
crashing into one another—
with the force of newly born
stars.

There are floor-thrown pieces—shards
strewn throughout the
wide and rounded rims of the universe.
No amount of supernova glue
can offer repair.

But sometimes I see such
new and lovely things
born of all our breaking.

Plunge and Rise

What wild seas today!
White-cresting waves and lashing
sheets of rain against the troughs.
How I long for the wings of an albatross,
crafted for the battery of wind,
their wide sweep,
their gale-cupping-curl,
their endless plunge and rise—
and rise—
and rise—

Perfectionism

The constant pursuit of excellence,
eternally chasing flaw's absence
winds me, spiralling, ever inward,
and to what end?
Forward motion remains elusive,
exclusive thinking narrowing my reasoning
while my mind fills with heartaches.
In favour of balance, I would be so much
better for making gentle mindful mistakes.

Those Three Words

I throw love around like confetti,
pocketing it in case of emergencies, or just, Tuesdays.
I have undoubtedly made people uncomfortable
from time to time, (myself included)
unaccustomed, to the ease of those three little words.
But I am always wondering—
What if those words are the most necessary,
the most required for survival?
And what if we are all barely surviving
most days? Does it not, then, measure and not cheapen,
to speak them freely, casually, gently, sincerely?
Are we not all human, truly, and desperate for more than
commentary about the weather?
It's raining.
I love you.

Borrowed

I wish there were lender cards for hearts.
'Here. You can put your stamp on this.
Then we would know who holds us.'
And for exactly how long. Perhaps
we could prepare a little better.
I think I'd write 'No late fees'
on the flyleaf. Just in case
someone decided
to read me
forever.

Do I Love You?

Darling, I've used all my words
telling you so.
But perhaps I spoke too softly.
I am only one person, after all.
So now then, also this:
I've spent days nurturing
this starter by the hearth,
keeping the fire warm
and burning so it would rise,
double in size.
And then I added flour and water
and salt—to feed and flavour.
And I waited, working
overnight once, twice.
And now here at midnight
I am baking bread
for you.

Rose-Colored Glasses

Perhaps you imagine me naive
to see the world this way—
light-limned, and star-sprayed
always one breath away from resurrection.
I'll make no objection to more sombre views.
Honestly, I live there too, more often than you think.
Which is why I choose—
in the cold, stark darkness before light catches
the rim of the horizon,
to persistently pick up these glasses
and open my eyes.

Warming

'Can I have it in a cup for here?' I ask,
pointing to the ceramic mug,
none of

this paper nonsense
reminds me of fragility and the way things
are prone to disintegration if you don't hurry—hurry—hurry.
I need to wrap myself around

a slightly slower pace
lends itself nicely to noticing and I am tired of missing
what matters in favour of what is so urgently

now
I am mostly interested in holding my own hands
around this mug and warming
parts of my heart that have been cold
for too long.

Still Here

I go down to the edge
of the frozen field,
(which is actually a lake)
(which is actually the
cupped palms of the earth)

and stand silent.
The waiting water is also quiet
(beneath the snow)
(beneath the ice)
(beneath the dark bowl of the sky)

We are the same
(both other than what we seem)
(both weighted by the illusion)
longing for Spring.

Swimming Laps on Saturday Mornings

Saturday mornings at the pool are my favourite.
Frequented by the silver set who out-swim me
more often than not, and are unashamed
of their bodies in suits, in public, or of mine.
We chat about grandkids and their coffee friends,
and health—something none of them take for granted.
The older gentleman who swims at 10 a.m. always brings
his portable speaker, and streams
a wide musical repertoire into the pool area.
Billie Holiday, Billie Eilish, and Billy Joel,
Celine Dion and her eternal heart,
classical cello concertos, and classic rock…
He doesn't swim laps so much as dances down his lane,
hands in the air, body free from gravity.
And me: a captive audience,
grateful for every shared song and smile,
on these Saturday morning miles.

Requirements

I refuse to sit here silently and listen to you preach
while my heart deteriorates and my mind unwinds
beneath the weight of the requirements you've
imposed, (you, not God), to ensure your pews remain full
and your plates plump. Meanwhile, my existence
crumbles beneath the weight of eternal life and
the power your version of God withholds from those
who have not repented well enough to be well.
Hell, (according to you) will be full of people like me,
starving and willing enough to lick knife blades
while the keys of the kingdom are dropped
into the pockets of gatekeepers.
Meanwhile, God is out here on the step sitting
with the rest of us. And I swear by all that is whole
and holy, salvation was meant for
Every. Single. One. Of. Us.
regardless of how whole our hearts are
when we arrive.

Spiral

This inward curl
used to catch me by surprise.
The unconscious drawing closer
and quieter and deeper.
I used to imagine I was flawed—
for winding inward to rest
before finding strength to wind back out again.
But, I have found I am far from alone.
The fronds of ferns, and
the rush of white-crested waves.
Snails, and the growth-rings of trees,
hurricanes, the wrap of rose petals,
fingerprints, and quiet churning river eddies.
Even our lovely, unfathomable, star-freckled galaxy
is a spiral. For perhaps, the universe itself
must curl in
to rest.

Warm Spell

The reach of a February warm spell draws
snow from rooftops, and red squirrels from their dens,
and me from my own hibernation,
out into the late afternoon.
I am not immune to the certainty of more snow
or to cold in negative increments.
But for this bright moment, I swing my arms, and trace
deer trails through the woods—their heart-shaped prints
like love notes in the soft ground.
And when I press my palms
against the waist of that far-flung maple,
catching the rush of wind somewhere far overhead,
it occurs to me that we are all drawing up lifeblood—
red squirrels, and deer, and maple trees, and me.
For nothing is impervious to
the whispered invitation
of this solstice-tilting north.

Retrostective

'Do you remember?'
This is how I usually begin.
At the end of things. Because in
this completion
they make the most sense to me.
Neatly wrapped and packaged
in tiny totalities, where the messy middle
has already been lived through—said and done.
Some part of me must need to know
that both the lovely
and the valleyed stories of my life
find finish and fulfilment
in recollective retellings.
Only there,
I can determine outcomes
and reserve these better
endings.

Joyfully

with flowing grace
you boldly displayed
every aspect of
you elaborated your history
from the challenges and resolutions
of your youth
all the way to the day
of our connection
then looked at me
with loving eyes that saw right through
and gently removed
the chains and walls
that I had installed
around my soul to use
for protection
hand in hand
joyfully
we began our journey
in a new direction

Drive

Stasis equals madness.

The minutes click by—
pain resides
settling into the fallow fields
of the placid.
If the universe
and the line of time
were truly infinity
what would you believe?

Beauty
calls for boldness
while adequacy
tries to roll us
into degradation
feeding others' greed
with our degeneration.

The source of all wisdom
is not philosophy
but base human need.

Desire provides
the inciting heat.

Distant

The electricity is spotty tonight
it's difficult
to get the temperature in the room right
the horns still beeping continuously
in the streets outside
as my hotel room goes from light
to dark to light

it's a lazy night
and I really don't care if there's power
or if I'm camping
unless the heat rises
past my personal ceiling

but right now
for some unknown reason
nothing
is really bothering me—

I'm staring at the stars
and what I'm guessing
is Venus

and not really phased
by any earthly feelings.

Light Fog

It's dark in this room—
it's a quarter past late
and my brain
is awake
though my body reels
in exhaustion

and I'm staring
out the window silently gazing
at the metro train
which is steadily pacing
its weary way
home to the terminal station

other than that
nothing seems to be moving—

just the city lights
twinkling
in this post-midnight haze

other than that
I sit thinking of you—
lost reminiscing
of those bright sunny days.

Downpour

I wanted so badly
for it to rain last night.

For the skies
to split wide open
and drop an ocean
onto the parking lot.

You told me
don't get my expectations
too high

(Believe me—
you're the only high
I've got)

The heat
and the pressure
on the edges of this city
have risen to the oppressive—

I think we all need
a downpour of relief—
a showering of life.

I wanted so badly
for it to rain last night.

Elevated

Swooping and sweeping
the eagles
soar
so closely
past the restaurant window
high up on the fifteenth floor

riding
the rising heat
from the crowded streets
outside

the waiter
is dressed impeccably
as he arrives
with a glass of whisky
on a tray

the customer scowls and says arrogantly
you sure took your time

the waiter gives a courteous smile
and sets the drink down
silently

in my eyes
I've never seen anyone
look more dignified.

Gentle Rain

thunder cracked
and lightning flashed
across the desolate
desert of sky
last night
finally
the rain poured down
powerful and delightful
this morning
the air is fresh and cool
the flowers
have blossomed so thick in the trees
that now the petals
themselves
fall like a gentle shower
to the ground
surrounding
and enhancing your beauty
with beauty

Life Bursts Forward

Winter has not yet released its
cold grip yet spring cannot sit idly waiting.

The first time the temperature rises above freezing
the blossoms shout forth from the cherry trees.

A sea of green sprouts blissfully
from yielding fields and wild as a child I
run bare assed through the grass.

My frozen hibernation in a tomb is over:
I rise and fuel those fires of primal energy,
slurp lustfully every wild blackberry I find,
and suck the sweet juice from the nibble clover.

I bury my thirsty face deep in the lap
of the scandalous wildflowers licking
and smelling the petals that seductively
lure me off that cold paved path.

Life bursts forward and so do I, and I
cannot take a step back.

Fuel

The body
is a temple—
not a tomb.

Fragrance
taste
touch
music
view
every sensation
is purest fuel.

Don't allow your light
to be buried in dirt
or trapped within caves
of mundane concerns.

Burn bright,
the light
of the internal fire.

Nourish the soul
with the flames of desire

Pulse

chemical
instinctive

rhythmical
yet free

a beat that escapes
the chains
of the metronome

activates
an energy
all its own

feral
innate

primal
and deep

the music of souls
in natural harmony

Always Close

I'm not that far
from downtown,
but also for sure
I know that I'm
not distant
from a deer
right now.

A woodpecker or an owl
I guarantee you
is near—
I don't have to see
these transcendent creatures:
I can hear
their pulse—
feel their heartbeats
drumming in my ears.

Vital

The wild birds
missed me—
they swarmed
my front yard
upon my return.

Sparrows and robins
and the couple
of cardinals: I like
to call them husband and wife.

They follow me
as I walk the streets
of my neighbourhood
snapping photos

I was gone for about
a couple of weeks: they scolded me a bit
while I tossed out
that first cup of seed.

Sometimes
(I've got to admit)
it's nice to be needed.

Roadmap

Driving
along the highway of life
anything
beyond the horizon
is faith.

The trees and flowers
that line the sides
of the road
are merely
indicators
of what may come our way.

I stood face to face
with you: that time
together translates
into a roadmap.

Day by day
I continue forward
I cannot stray
left or right
from the path.

Early Weekend

The trees
are beginning
to sprout little leaves
tiny shoots
of brilliant green
that call to me
on this Friday afternoon
begging me
to leave this straight-lined room
I can't pay my rent
if I always start the weekend
early: following the trends
that every season brings
but Lord
how I want to
turn off my computer
and dance barefoot
in this glorious spring

Relevance

We speak
words
in the same manner as birds
celebrating noisily

Singing
about what has already
come to be

Spoken
into existence
even before the beginning

The birth
of what was
so long ago conceived

Preexisting
this instant of eternity
shaped capriciously
into physical bodies

I am you
you are me

under our feet
the pain
of this world
falls away
into obscurity.

Vision

I carry the moon
in a glass of water,
I hold your beauty
in the back of my eyes.

I see your soul
in every sunrise.

I hear the way
your necklace sways,
I dance
with the rhythm your heartbeat resonates.

The fragrance
of your luxurious hair
flips my brain
over
and then,
just for fun,
flips it over again.

You ask
for me to tell you the truth.

It's one simple line:

I see you.

Nothing

I have stood,
cold
in desire.
I have knelt,
trembling
in want.

Yearning,
burning in desperation,
my hands weak with reaching
yet touching naught.

There's a difference
between needing
and emptiness.

A shift
subtle as a rippling

on a lake,
monumental
as an earthquake.

Transmuting
within the arms of the void.

From nothing to discernment
to fulfilment to joy.

Immersion

I burn my skin
in the summer heat,
in the winter
I shiver naked and freezing.

Hungry
I tap every crumb on the table
and lick my fingers clean.

Thirsty
I drink this cup of coffee right down
to the bitter grinds then spoon them up and chew.

I adore
every heavenly millimetre of you.
I sleep
for no other reason than to wake to you.

Alone
I dream of you,
together
I am you.

Purification

With cutting board
and sharp knife I cut away
any edge
of the vegetable
which lacks perfection
and unceremoniously
throw it away.

Anything painful
is not love
and everything which is love
causes no pain.

With peace
and contemplation I remove
any part of being in love
which does not fill me

with joy
and I amplify
what remains.

Love Is a Stream

dive in whole
dip in a toe
skim a rock
wash your clothes
float on the surface
ride the waves
abandon your cares
they will float away
splash in it
swim in it
paddle a canoe
let the sun-sparkled ripples
massage and caress you
you don't need to receive
every drop
there is no goal

love is a stream
there is nothing to hold
love is not the water
love is the flow

PROSENJIT NATH is a technocrat, poet, and writer whose literary enthusiasm pervaded every facet of his existence. An ardent passion for poetry and creative expression complements his technological career. His works exude sensitivity and astuteness, mirroring his profound inner life. As a lifelong literary aficionado, Prosenjit makes a lasting impact as both a visionary and a wordsmith.